<u>DEDICATION</u>

The book is dedicated to **my Father**... "To the world you may be one person, but to me you are the world"

PREFACE

In an increasingly globalized world and the changing paradigm of urbanized living the demand for Hospitality and Tourism has increased manifold the world over, this book speaks for itself. It it has been felt that there is a growing demand for trained housekeeping personnel who can give a professional touch to housekeeping wherever they work in hotels, guest houses, hospitals, offices, shopping complex resorts, etc. This book will enable all learners to give that professional edge to their housekeeping skills. It has been a deliberate effort to keep the language used in this student's book as simple as possible. Necessary pictorial illustrations and formats have been included to help the students to understand the concepts without any difficult.

TABLE OF CONTENT

1. Introduction

Introduction to housekeeping department.

Meaning, Definition & Importance of Housekeeping Department

Role of Housekeeping in hospitality industry

2. Lay out & Organizational Structure

Layout of Housekeeping department

Organizational Structure of Housekeeping department (Small, Medium & large)

Interdepartmental relationship (emphasis on Front office & Maintenance)☐

Relevant sub section

3. Staffing in Housekeeping Department

Role of key personnel in Housekeeping department

Job description & Job specification of Housekeeping staff (Executive Housekeeper, Floor supervisor, Public area supervisor etc. .

4. Planning work of Housekeeping department

Identifying Housekeeping department

Briefing & Debriefing

Control desk (importance , role , coordination)

Role of Control Desk during emergency

Duty Rota & work schedule

Files with format used in Housekeeping department.

5. Hotel Guest Room

Types of room-definition

Standard layout (single ,double ,twin ,suit)

☐ Difference between Smoking & Non Smoking room"s

☐ Barrier free room"s

Furniture / Fixture / Fitting / Soft Furnishing /Accessories / Guest Supplies /Amenities in a guest room Layout corridor& floor Pantry

6. Cleaning Science

Characteristics of good cleaning agent

Application of cleaning agent

Types of cleaning agent

Cleaning products

Cleaning equipments

☐ Classification and types of equipment with Diagram"s (Mops , dusters , pushers, mechanical squeeze, vacuum cleaner ,shampooing machine) with their care and uses

CHAPTER-1

Introduction

A CONCISE HISTORY OF HOTEL KEEPING

In medieval Europe, before the advent of the hotel industry, monasteries traditionally offered hospitality to travellers. Donations were made voluntarily. In those days, the Christian monasteries, which were mostly wealthy organizations, functioned to a certain extent as charitable institutions. Their main aim, however, was to offer hospitality for pilgrims and this purpose, the monasteries were usually located at the site of holy places.

The first commercial venture in the field of hotel keeping was the European inns, specifically designed as profit making businesses. With the advent of stagecoaches, wayside inns sprung up between towns and these were usually larger than the city inns. The mode of transport throughout history has greatly influenced hotel keeping. With the advent of railways came station hotels; with the advent of aircrafts airport hotels were built, motor ways and extensive road travel necessitated the construction of motels while boats and ships are, in fact, floating hotels.

TRADITION OF HOSPITALITY IN INDIA

In the traditional literature of India, there are many references which reflect that hospitality was deeply ingrained in the culture. It was offered on an individual or village basis and was not organized as in the present times.

Later, Buddhist monasteries took up the task of providing food and lodging for travellers. It is noted that in the reign of Chandragupta Maurya, inns and guest houses were established. Later, universities established their own guest houses. Dharamshalas were also widely built near Hindu holy cities.

With the construction of the Grand Trunk Road in the Moghul period, inns or SERAIS became a national feature. Most of these establishments were also involved in the postal service as mail was sent on horseback via the Grand Trunk Road. This road was responsible for huge increase in the number of inns in India.

During the British rule in India, DAK bungalows came into being as lodges for government officials on tour as well as for tourists when accommodation was available.

VARIOUS TYPES OF HOTELS AND SERVICES OFFERED

A hotel is a 'home away from home' for guests.

The basic definition of a hotel is — 'A place that offers accommodation, food and beverage for sufficient money to enable the hotel to make a profit.'

The three main services that hotels have to provide are:

• Accommodation (main source of revenue generation)

• Food

• Beverages

Hotels are graded according to the facilities they offer in terms of space, furnishings and amenities such as swimming pools, leisure centres, and so on. They are marked from five star to one star, according to the size or the degree of luxury they offer, and to some extent, based on design and location. Five star is the highest and most luxurious among hotels and one star implies the simplest style. The governments of each country rates their hotels and presently, there is no international star-rating system.

In most cases, city hotels are business hotels catering to the business class travellers and provide conference facilities and a business centre with typing, telex work, Internet and general secretarial services. However, in certain ways some city hotels are also tourist hotels. Tourist hotels offer travel agency and at times airline office facilities and souvenir shops within their building.

Accommodation facilities in hotels tend to form the largest and usually, the most profitable part of the hotel. The housekeeping department that takes care of all the rooms, is often, the largest department in a hotel. The rooms offered as accommodation for travellers are individual units of a bedroom with an attached bathroom. Many hotels also offer suites which means units of more than one room that are not all bedrooms and mostly includes a sitting room.

Hotels offer laundry and dry-cleaning facilities for clothes and shoe-polishing facilities to make the guests as comfortable as possible by offering all the necessary services.

Along with offering accommodation, hotels also offer bar and restaurant facilities. Room service is also usually provided whereby guests can have a tray or trolley brought to their room. Bars sell alcoholic beverages, soft drinks and sometimes snacks.

Most hotel offer guests the choice of a coffee shop or a more expensive and speciality restaurant(s). The more expensive or larger hotels offer more dining choices.

Banqueting, meeting and private party facilities are available in most hotels. Revenue can be generated from conferences, weddings, meetings and seminars. A lot of hotels often have an arcade of shops. Newspaper, sweets, cigarettes, souvenirs, jewellery, clothes and leather goods' shops are some of the common sights in most hotels. The hotel may run the shops themselves, but it is more usual to contract out the premises to shopkeepers.

Hairdressing saloons for men and women are also a normal feature of large hotels.

A health club is a part of resort hotels. It includes a swimming pool with a small pool kept aside for children. An exercise gymnasium, massage rooms, hydrotherapy, sauna and Turkish bath are the most common provisions. Hydrotherapy, which means water therapy, can be a Jacuzzi, which is a water massage tank or bath. It can also be a foam generating water bath. In case of hot springs and sulphur springs, it uses that special water. Sauna bath is dry heat while Turkish baths use wet heat. An exercise gymnasium usually has special equipment for exercise workouts such as exercise static bicycle, weightlifting equipment, etc.

Some hotels with large garden facilities provide jogging tracks. Often there is an early morning jog and exercise session followed by a quick swim and a health conscious breakfast. In many Indian hotels, yoga is included among the facilities of the health club and is very popular with foreigners. The health club can be used by hotel residents and usually by outside guests who pay a club membership fee. One also pays for all the facilities utilized each time. Normally, around the swimming pool one provides sun lounges, sometimes also called chaise lounges.

If a hotel has beach facilities then it is normal to offer drinks on beaches. Beach hotels offer boating, sailing, surfing, windsurfing and often water skiing facilities.

A nightclub with entertainment, dancing and at times, dining as well as drinking facilities feature in many hotels.

Discotheques are another normal facility for dancing and are provided with modern music for young people with special lighting effects.

At the desk area or reception of a hotel, apart from check-in and check-out facilities, there is usually an information counter, facilities for exchanging foreign currency and travellers cheques and often, a hospitality desk.

These are the basic facilities that hotels offer to their guests. Hotels try to make the surrounding as pleasant as possible through nice colour schemes, attractive furnishing, a clean and well-kept building and an efficient and polite staff.

In India, the five star luxury hotels are usually excellent but the other grades are also getting more business. The revenue potential in three star to five star is enormous and more concentration is being given to them.

An alternative to the five-star hotels in other countries are the medium priced hotels, which are run by reputable

companies with simpler furnishings and services, e.g., only breakfast included in room service and with a limited menu.

In other countries, due to high labor costs, services are curtailed in this way to make the room rate cheaper for the guests. There may be a smaller number of dining choices or bars in such hotels. However, as cleanliness, quality of food and services are still the benchmarks, some have suites to offer guests.

Budget hotels are even simpler than the medium priced bracket and usually offer no suites and no room service. Despite being very simple they still have clean and attractive furnishings. Dining facilities are usually one coffee-shop type restaurant, but again with good service and food.

It is possible to provide attractive and clean accommodation to guests by reducing certain services to lower costs. Cheaper hotels do not need to be dirty or provide terrible food. In fact, in many parts of the world this is the most profitable and fastest-growing sector.

Motels mean hotels on motorways and are in the developing stage in our country. In other countries, where nearly everyone has a car, there are more travellers. Motels should maintain proper cleanliness and pleasant surroundings. Often, one has parking directly outside the unit, which is very convenient for travellers. Motels usually provide a petrol/diesel filling station facility.

Motels are in fact transit type hotels situated near the airport or railway station and guests usually stay one night. So, one has to provide much wardrobe space or drawers and storage in the room.

Conference hotels tend to be a mixture of medium priced type rooms but with suites and public areas resembling more a luxury hotel. This is to facilitate the delegates at conferences to meet important people. In such hotels, one will find large as well as smaller meeting facilities and similar banqueting rooms also.

Hotels can offer varied facilities for their guests and there are great differences in the types of hotels. When it comes to hotel keeping there are no hard and fast rules regarding what is correct or otherwise.

ORGANIZATION OF HOTELS

The organization of each hotel is slightly different because of the size, type of hotel and the layout.

Smaller hotels tend to have less specialized departments than larger ones and in smaller hotels there can be a doubling-up of jobs, e.g., the receptionist may also have to clean other areas or people cleaning rooms may also have to clean other areas such as banqueting rooms.

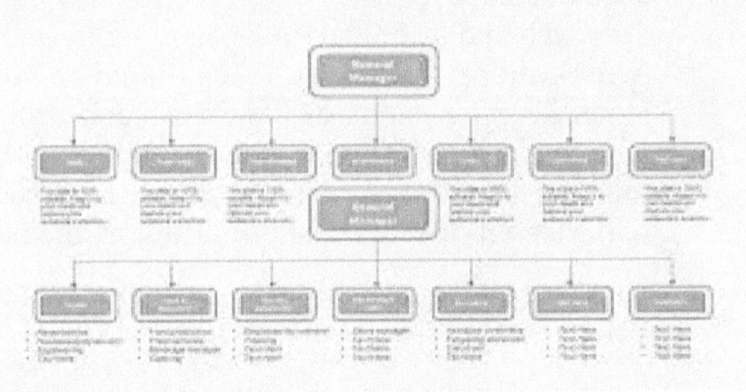

HOUSEKEEPING IN HOTELS

Hotels are commercially operated for the guests who have a choice of where to stay and pay for the accommodation and services received. The housekeeper has to bear in mind that the guests must be attracted to the establishment, so marketing and selling are important factors. Further more amenities and services must be geared to meet the demands of the market to which the hotel caters.

Within hotels the housekeeping department provides cleaning and domestic services.

IMPORTANCE OF HOUSEKEEPING

Housekeeping is the most important department in a hotel, as people want to stay in a clean hotel. It is the biggest physical area in many hotels. Housekeeping is responsible for maintenance of a clean, pleasant and orderly environment.

The housekeeping department is the nerve centre of the hotel. It is responsible for cleanliness, maintenance and aesthetic upkeep of the hotel. It takes a well- organized approach and technical understanding to enable housekeeping to cope with the volume of work. Housekeeping standards have a direct bearing on forming an everlasting impression and impact in the mind of the guest. A clean hotel is the foremost requirement of every visitor putting up the hotel.

Standard cleanliness is the basic responsibility of the housekeeping department.

Repeat clientele and generation of maximum revenue depends upon the efficient and smooth running of the

housekeeping operation. To have such efficiency, there should be a proper network, so that maximum service can be provided to the guest and for this, each one should put in one's best efforts.

FUNCTIONS OF HOUSEKEEPING

The function of a hotel's housekeeping department is to provide, organize and control cleaning, linen and laundry and room servicing throughout the hotel. The standard of this work and particularly the type and amount of room servicing provided will depend upon the level of accommodation provided. The provision of these services will be reflected in the tariff for each room.

The main functions of housekeeping are to:

• Ensure cleanliness and comfort in a safe and secure environment

• Provide services economically and efficiently

• Promote the comfort of the guests, staff and visitors

• Assist in the maintenance of the fabric of the building, while contributing to a safe, healthy environment

ROLE OF HOUSEKEEPING IN THE HOSPITALITY INDUSTRY

• The housekeeping department is responsible for the cleanliness, maintenance and aesthetic appeal of the entire hotel.

• From the housekeeping point of view, hotels can be classified as small, medium and large hotels. Based on the level of service provided, hotels can be economy, mid-market and first class/luxury hotels.

• Economy hotels focus on meeting the most basic need of the guest by providing clean, comfortable and inexpensive rooms.

• Mid-market hotels appeal to the largest segment of travellers. They offer reasonably good service and may offer suite accommodation, i.e., the living room being separate from the bedroom. Kitchenette facilities are usually provided in suite rooms.

• Luxury hotels provide world-class services, up-scale food and beverage outlets, exquisite décor, concierge service, large banquet halls, etc. These hotels mostly cater to the rich and famous people. The guest rooms are well furnished and the art and décor is more expensive than other hotels.

• It is the housekeeping department that is responsible for cleaning the entire hotel as nothing sends a stronger message than the cleanliness of a hotel. The hotel's image can be made or unmade in the eyes of the guests by the staff of the housekeeping department, and thus their role is extremely important.

CHAPTER-2

LAYOUT AND ORGANIZATIONAL STRUCTURE

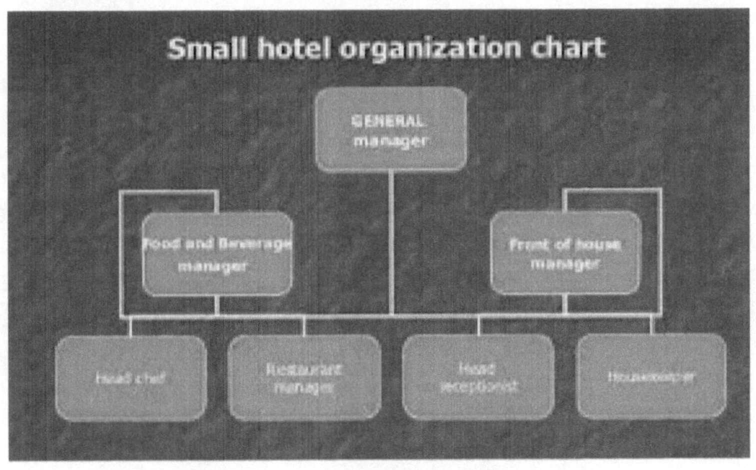

The housekeeping department in a hotel is responsible for the maintenance, cleanliness and aesthetic upkeep of the hotel. Just as the nomenclature signifies, the role of housekeeping is to keep a clean, comfortable and safe house. It is an extension of basic home-keeping multiplied into commercial proportions. Therefore, just as we enjoy keeping a SPARKLING HOME for ourselves and guests who visit us at home, the housekeeping department takes pride in keeping the hotel clean and comfortable, to create a HOME AWAY FROM HOME.

The concept of housekeeping is simplistic but when one considers maintaining a HOUSE OF SEVERAL HUNDRED ROOMS and NUMEROUS PUBLIC AREAS, the task becomes gigantic. It takes a well-organized approach and technical understanding to enable housekeeping to cope with the volume of work.

A hotel survives on the sale of rooms, food and beverage and other minor operating services such as the laundry, health clubs, etc. The largest margin of profit comes from room sales in a hotel, because a room, once made, can be sold over and over again. A good hotel operation ensures optimal room sales to being in the maximum profit.

The room sale is dependent on, apart from several other things, i.e., the quality of room decor, room facilities, cleanliness of the room and how safe it is. To make a room appealing to a guest is the task of housekeeping which has to ensure the basic human needs of comfort and security.

BASIC LAYOUT OF THE HOUSEKEEPING DEPARTMENT

There is no ideal universal model for the layout of a housekeeping department. The basic layout differs from hotel to hotel and is dependent upon its size and physical space limitation. There are so many functional rooms in a hotel. Some of these are linen room, linen and uniform room, tailor shop, laundry, security, supplies store, flower room, etc. It is important not to ask for space more than is required because space is limited and entails cost. As a thumb rule, the following spaces would have to be provided for the essential activities of the department

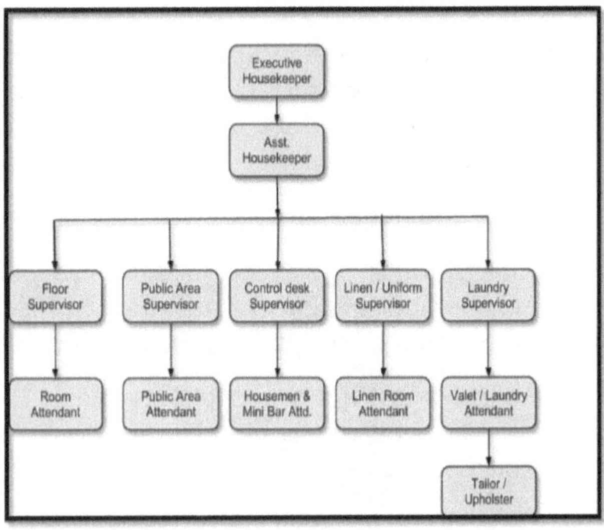

AREAS OF RESPONSIBILITY OF THE HOUSEKEEPING DEPARTMENT

1. Housekeeper's office: This is the main administration centre for the department. It must be an independent cabin to provide the Housekeeper with silence to plan out her work. It will also provide her with the privacy to counsel her staff or hold departmental meetings. It should preferably be a glass-panelled office to give her a view of what is happening outside her office.

2.   **Desk control room:** This is the main communication centre of housekeeping. It would normally adjoin the Housekeeper's Office. The Desk Control Room should have a desk and a chair with preferably more than one telephone. It should have a large notice board to pin up staff schedules, day-to-day instructions, etc. The Desk Control Room is the point where all staff report for duty and check out at the duty end.

3.   **Guest rooms/floors:** Room attendants and floor supervisors are responsible for the cleanliness, maintenance and security of guest rooms and the surrounding areas.

4. **Public areas**:

FRONT OF THE HOUSE AREAS: Lobby, shopping arcade, restaurants, banquet rooms, health club, swimming pool, recreation areas, parking area and compound area.

BACK OF THE HOUSE AREAS: Basement, all operating departments (except kitchen which is cleaned by the kitchen stewards), service areas, staff locker rooms and offices.

Thorough cleaning of all public areas is usually done in the night.

Linen and uniform room: The housekeeping department is responsible for the functioning, repairs and renewal of linen and for maintaining proper inventory and stock records of all linen items. It includes room linen, restaurant linen, uniforms and soft furnishings.

Laundry:

ON-PREMISES LAUNDRY: If the laundry is on the premises, then the guest laundry from the rooms is directly collected and delivered by the laundry valet.

However, all hotel linen is first collected in the linen room and then given to the laundry for washing.

OFF-PREMISES LAUNDRY: The laundering of both guest and hotel linen is done on contract by an external laundry. All the linen is collected in the linen room from where it is given to the laundry for washing.

Uniform room: This rootstock the uniforms in current use. Smaller hotels may choose to combine the Uniform Room with the Linen Room. A separate Uniform Room depends on the volume of uniforms in circulation. The only difference would be that the uniform room would have adequate hanging facilities as many uniforms are best maintained when hung.

8. Tailors room: This room is kept for house tailors who attend to the stitching and mending work of linen and uniforms. If the house policy is to contract out all tailoring and mending work, the tailor's room could be avoided.

9. Heavy equipment stores: This will be room to store bulky items, such as shampoo machines, vacuum cleaners, ladders for chandelier or window cleaning, etc. The room should be clean and dry. It should also securely locked to avoid stealing or pilferage by other departments.

10. Greenhouse: As horticulture comes under housekeeping normally, a greenhouse to foster specialized plants is necessary for the garden areas. The greenhouse should have wooden racks to store pots, etc.

11. Shoeshine: Resident guests are given this service by room attendants on a complimentary basis. Some hotels may have a shoe shine machine installed in the corridor.

12. Florist: This could either be given out on the contract or an employee of the housekeeping department could do the flower arrangements required for VIP rooms, suites, executive offices, public areas and for the florist shop. Any banquet requirements such as the backdrop for a wedding, etc., is done on contract.

13. Special requests: Extra room compliments and supplies, first-aid kit (no oral medication without the advice of the house doctor) irons, a hot-water bottle, ice-packs, thermometer, hairdryers, etc., are given at no extra cost for guest use. A request for extra beds, however, should be routed through the Front Office since the guest would be charged extra for it.

14. Babysitting: If a guest requests this facility, chambermaids may undertake to do babysitting after their regular shift or professional baby sitters are arranged for by the housekeeping department. The guest is charged by the hour.

15. Lost and found: Any guest article found in rooms or public areas is kept in the possession of the housekeeping department until a guest claims for it. Perishables – 24 hrs, valuables – 6 months to 1 year, of not much value – 3 to 6 months.

Lost and Found

16. Contract services: Pest control, carpet shampoo, laundry, florist, landscaping, cleaning the outer façade of the building, etc., are some of the cleaning services that are done on contract by the housekeeping department.

17. Refurbishment and redecoration: Refurbishment implies complete renovation where all the soft furnishings are changed and the furniture too may be changed or redone. It is usually undertaken once in 3–5 years floor wise.Redecoration, on the other hand, is done on a need basis as and when required – piece/area wise, e.g., redoing the upholstery of a sofa or changing a set of curtains as it is stained or worn out.

18. Any special decoration: Parties hosted by the hotel, e.g., Christmas Dance, New Year Ball, Navratri, etc., or food festivals, which require special décor is looked after the housekeeping department in coordination with the Food and Beverage Department.

Purchase: The executive housekeeper is responsible for the purchase of cleaning equipment, cleaning agents, linen, soft furnishings, uniforms, room complimentary and supplies. All large chain hotels may have a central purchase department through which room supplies are obtained on a monthly/quarterly basis. This ensures consistency of room supplies in all hotels of the chain.

Budgeting: The executive housekeeper presents the annual budget in January for the forthcoming budgeting financial year. The factors to be considered while drawing up the budget are previous year budget + 10% inflation + refurbishment plans + any other capital purchase + expected occupancy.

Duty rotas/rosters: The executive housekeeper decides to shift timings and the day off of all housekeeping employees. Also, leave sanctioning, overtime and statement of attendance is sent by the executive housekeeper to the Personnel Department at the end of each month for calculating the payroll of the housekeeping staff.

Interview, selection, induction, training and performance appraisal: The executive housekeeper is responsible for the final selection and training of all housekeeping staff. Performance appraisals are drawn up annually for permanent employees, quarterly for probationers and monthly for trainees.

INTER-DEPARTMENT COOPERATION

All the departments in a hotel have to cooperate and coordinate to attain the final objective, viz. guest satisfaction.

Housekeeping works very closely with

• Reception

• Maintenance

• Food and beverage department

Cooperation is essential among these departments

HOUSEKEEPING AND RECEPTION

The housekeeping department is the product manufacturer and reception department is the seller.

Information supplied by the reception to housekeeping:

Exchange of information regarding room status

Exchange of information regarding servicing of rooms

Occupancy forecast information

Night report

Daily VIP arrival list and in-house guests

Daily anticipated departure list

Long-term forecast of VIP arrivals

Group rooming lists

Room changes

Arrivals' lists

Information was given by housekeeping to reception

1. Housekeeping report

2. Check out/ready rooms information

3. Sleepouts

4. Out-of-order rooms

5. Anticipated check out which have not been let

6. Unusual observations

7. Special cleaning schedules

HOUSEKEEPING AND MAINTENANCE

Information was given by housekeeping to maintenance

 Maintenance requests

Special cleaning programmes

Information was given by maintenance to housekeeping

1. Special preventive maintenance schedules

2. Special equipment servicing

HOUSEKEEPING AND FOOD AND BEVERAGE DEPARTMENT

Information was given by housekeeping to food and beverage department

 Linen and uniform inventory plans xviii.
Shampooing/special cleaning of public area information
Information given by the food and beverage department to housekeeping

1. Banqueting diary forecast

HOUSEKEEPING AND OTHER DEPARTMENTS

With Laundry

1. Cleaning of guest laundry, hotel linen and staff uniform

2. Close cooperation between the linen room and laundry

With Security

1. Prevention of theft, fire or other accidents in hotel

2. Crime prevention

3. Reporting of any suspicious person to security promptly

Purchase/Stores

1. Timely availability of various cleaning equipment and agents

2. Guest supplies and amenities

Computer Center

1. Information exchange regarding lost and found

2. Guest reservations

3. Overstay, etc.

Accounts

1. Salary disbursement

2. Sanctioning funds for various housekeeping related purchases, etc.

Personnel

1. Recruitment, training and maintaining a personal file of staff

2. Leave record, overtime, etc.

Horticulture

1. Flower arrangement

2. Bouquet preparation

CHAPTER-3

STAFFING IN HOUSEKEEPING DEPARTMENT

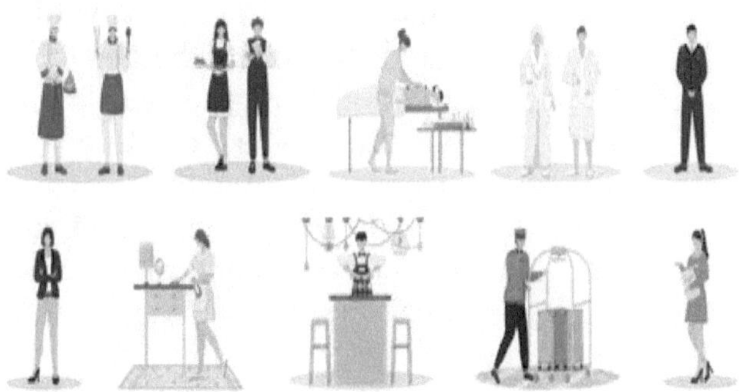

OUTLINE OF DUTIES AND FUNCTIONS OF THE STAFF IN A HOUSEKEEPING DEPARTMENT

Executive Housekeeper

Smaller hotels often give the title of head housekeeper and nowadays some large hotels are using the title director of housekeeping services or director of guests services. Traditionally, this position was occupied by a lady but nowadays men are found in supervisory and executive positions in housekeeping departments.

The person in this position is ultimately responsible for all the work and staffing of the department. Naturally, the organization of work and people play a large part in a successful operation. The executive housekeeper must also have the sound technical knowledge and remain updated on new developments in the industry. For this job, a person must be a good manager and must be able to conceptualize plans as well as be active because one needs to check the work and standard of the staff.

Executive Assistant Housekeeper

In some cases, the title of executive assistant is given. If there is more than one assistant, normally a senior one is appointed to depute on the holidays or in the absence of the executive housekeeper. Large hotels often have more than one assistant and divide up various responsibilities among them, e.g., while one is responsible for the floors and office work connected with staff, another may be responsible for public areas, stores, supplies and reordering of cleaning materials and products. Another may take charge of staff training and maintaining training records. The assistant/s checks on the work of the staff in her area and ensures that correct and appropriate standards are being maintained.

Supervisors

There are supervisors for the rooms and also for public areas. The linen room also has a supervisor. In many hotels, there are at least two senior supervisors as both the jobs entail more responsibility than room-checking on the floors.

Floor Supervisor

They are sometimes called floor housekeepers. They check the work of the room-attendants. They ensure that the rooms and all areas including corridors and service-rooms are cleaned to the required standard. They have also to ensure that the correct supplies of towels and complimentary items, e.g., soap, notepads and envelopes are in each room. If the work is not up to the standard, they have to ensure it is re-done.

These people are in charge of deciding when a room is ready to enable reception to relet it to a new guest, so they have to communicate with the reception on this matter. In some hotels, all this information is conveyed to the housekeeping office first and then to the reception.

Generally, they are in charge of approximately 60 to 70 rooms each depending on the size of the floors and the standards of the hotels.

Public Area Supervisor

Sometimes know as a banqueting housekeeper, she is responsible for controlling the work in the public areas. These include banqueting areas in a hotel with a busy banqueting schedule. This is a very responsible position because the banqueting/ meeting room area must be cleaned before the event and often again quickly for another event later the same day. Thus, correct timing is essential in the banqueting diary.

Evening Supervisor/s

Evening supervisors are in charge of checking and controlling the work in the evening shift in guest rooms and public areas. Their duty covers the following areas:

1. To check all function areas, restaurants and public cloakrooms at regular intervals.

2. To check all the guest rooms and releasing them to the reception.

3. To check all the log entries, checking on double lock and 'Do Not Disturb' rooms.

4. To handover to the night supervisor

5. To ensure that the evening service has been given in the guest rooms.

Night Supervisor

They are in charge of the night shift, who very rarely do rooms. When immediately required they offer checkout, followed by immediate check-in (this is rare in the middle of the night). The majority of the work of the night shift is the cleaning of the public areas (which are at their quietest at night) and office and back areas also. Often, this position is held by men and can even be a sort of head

houseman position in smaller hotels.

Their work profile includes:

1. Supervising thorough scrubbing and cleaning of all public areas.

2. Checking of departure rooms required for new arrivals.

3. Handover the night report to the morning desk supervisor.

Room Attendants

Room attendants are responsible for the cleaning and service of a section of rooms and bathrooms which varies depending on the type of hotel and the number of rooms on each floor. In more luxurious hotels, they serve fewer rooms as each room is more complicated and takes longer to service. On average, it is between 12 to 16 rooms to each section. Room attendants also clean corridors and service back areas. Some hotels have separate people for this.

Public Area Cleaners/Houseman

This department usually looks after the banqueting and public area cleaning. Some hotels have housemen to clean corridors. They also are used for transporting linen and store, and supplying extra beds/cots and any heavy lifting duties and usually have to use quite a lot of machinery.

Many hotels appoint a few housemen especially for carpet-shampooing continuously in the rooms.

Most of the cleaning of the public areas is carried out at night.

Order-Taker/Clerk

The person is this position is in the housekeeping office to answer the telephone (remember in most hotels guests can directly dial housekeeping from the rooms). She also does clerical work and typing. There is usually one for the day shift and one for the evening shift and a floor supervisor does the reliever duty on their off days.

Storekeeper

Many large hotels have a storekeeper for housekeeping when necessary. Sometimes, they combine this with other duties, e.g., carpets and storekeeping.

Linen and Uniform Room

In some hotels, this is in two separate rooms and the case of large hotels, there are usually separate supervisors for each room.

Linen Room Supervisor

The supervisor is in charge of linen stock and uniforms too and records. All uniforms and linen are exchanged on a clean for dirty basis, to keep stock

that has been issued correctly. She is in charge of the work of the linen and uniforms attendants as well as tailor/s and/or seamstresses.

Linen and Uniform Attendants

They issue clean for dirty linen and sends all the soiled linen to the laundry and receives the clean and stores it on the shelves.

Tailors/s and Seamstress

These people do all the sewing and mending work. Most hotels buy their uniforms from a uniform manufacturer but some hotels sew them on their premises.

Laundry

Can be a separate department or part of housekeeping.

Laundry Chief or Manager

This person is in charge of the work and staff of the laundry and dry-cleaning unit. The manager has to cooperate with the linen room very closely and should have the organizational ability as well as technical knowledge of fabrics and products.

Shift Leaders

Shift leaders take charge of organizing the work of the shift when the laundry manager is not there, e.g., evening shift. He has to understand all aspects of the work and machinery.

Dry-Cleaning Supervisor

The dry-cleaning supervisor is in charge of the dry-cleaning unit. This position demands a thorough knowledge of fabrics and spotting (stain removal) and the use of chemicals and the cleaning machinery.

PERSONAL QUALITIES OF HOUSEKEEPING PERSONNEL

The professional housekeeper must have self-confidence as well as the ability to train, teach and motivate the people working in the department. Teaching requires dedication and the desire to help others learn and practice, a quality admired by the management because of its importance in housekeeping. Ambition too is important as it may lead to advancement to other departments, such as in housekeeping, or a more active role in management or to a bigger housekeeping job in a larger property.

High on the list of necessary traits for success are honesty, loyalty and sincerity. Honesty in relationship with the management, loyalty to employees, both within the department and throughout the company and sincerity to the housekeeping staff. Loyalty in the housekeeping department is needed to help increase turnover.

A housekeeper must have the poise to meet the unexpected crisis that arises so often. A liberal amount of tolerance and stability are also necessary. Being persuasive, able to present an idea or explain a need convincingly will help, whether it is engineering to repair a leak or request the laundry to stop folding sheets and start washing banquet cloth for a late scheduled dinner.

As for all hotels, one outstanding prerequisite is excellent physical health to endure the busy long working days; one so frequently experienced in hotels.

Leadership qualities are required especially for the executive housekeeper; he should be charismatic, meaning the force of her character and personality should be somewhat arresting and can motivate others. She should be firm, fair and friendly. She should have the abilities to plan, organize and to delegate the workloads. The ability to foresee and avert problems is essential. She must have an understanding of people and must be able to communicate to all levels. She needs to be cool, calm and collected in order not to cause panic and also to arrest any panic situation in others. Dedication to one's department, hotel and the whole management team, in general, is a powerful self-motivating force.

JOB ANALYSIS

It refers to the procedure used in collecting information about one specific job. The job analysis, which may be considered the process of studying a specific job, is the first procedure in acquiring overall information concerning a job.

Specimen job descriptions of an executive housekeeper, uniform or linen room supervisor, a room attendant, a cloakroom attendant, a night supervisor, a uniform or

a linen room attendant, a tailor, a head gardener, and gardeners are given in Formats below

The best way to gather information for a job description is by questioning and observing. Watch the present job holder at work and also interview him about his job or even have his questionnaire. Interview the job holder's supervisor. If there are trainees in the job, discovering their difficulties may also help to draw an accurate description of that job. Discuss the job with anyone else who is affected by the way the job is carried out.

GUIDELINES FOR PREPARING JOB DESCRIPTIONS:

1. Set out to be brief but accurate.

2. Describe the reason the job exists in one sentence under the head 'job function'.

3. Write the titles or appointments under the job supervisor and job subordinates.

4. List the main duties using the words 'assist', 'clear', 'check', 'inspect', etc.

5. Under relationships with other people, describe the essential relationships by referring to the appointment.

6. Under 'limits of authority', describe anything that limits the job holder's right to act, e.g., the amount of money he can spend without reference to a higher authority or is disciplining staff.

7. On completion of the job description, ask the present holder to look at it and check that it portrays a picture of his/her job.

The format I: Job Description of an Executive Housekeeper

Executive Housekeeper-. Organize the daily clearing and services of all

bedrooms and public rooms.

Supervise the collection, laundry and distribution of bed and table linen and staff uniforms.

Organize room service for early morning teas and breakfasts (up to 11.00 a.m. daily).

2. Requisition and control of the following stock:

(a) Cleaning materials

(b) Linen

(c) Room service crockery

3. Inspect staff accommodation with the hotel manager weekly.

4. Liaison with reception staff on accommodation services and security.

5. Plan and implement training of departmental staff in all relevant craft skills, social skills, fire drills and induction.

6. Assist and advise the managers in planning repairs and maintenance work, replacement of furnishings, fittings and equipment.

7. Assist and advise in the selection of housekeeping staff.

Job Requirements: 1. Responsibilities: Responsible for all activities and

operation of the housekeeping department.

2. Skills.

3. Equipment used.

Supervision: Job supervisor: Hotel Manager

Job subordinates: Floor housekeepers

Room maids

Part-time cleaners Laundry maids

Job Relationship: Contact maintenance staff, all departmental heads

and reception staff, fire inspection and fire equipment contractors, promotion to...

Qualification: As per Hotel norms.

Limits of authority: Cash up to certain amount on any one purchase.

Discipline: recommend dismissal of staff to the manager.

Format II: Job Description of a Uniform or Linen Room Supervisor

Job Code............

Job Title: Uniform/Linen Room Supervisor.

Reports to: Assistant Housekeeper.

Supervises Linen room attendants and helpers. Coordinates with: Laundry essentially but all other departments'

personnel.

Summary Job: 1. Schedule linen/uniform room staff.

2. Check periodically the condition of uniform and hotel linen.

3. Assign daily work to tailors.

4. Devise and maintain an effective control system to issue clean linen and uniforms.

5. Coordinate closely with the Laundry department to ensure timely supply of fresh uniforms and linen.

6. Conduct periodic inventories of linen and uniforms.

7. Ensure that all linen, uniforms needing stitching, mending are immediately attended to before being sent to the Laundry department.

8. Ensure that the Linen Room is kept neat and clean.

9. Ensure that all linen, uniforms, materials are neatly and systematically stacked and arranged.

10. Train the staff to perform their duties effectively and efficiently.

11. Maintain all relevant records in respect of material, uniforms/linen—their storage and movement.

Format III: Job Description of a Room Attendant

Job Title: RoomAttendant.

Reports to: Floor Supervisor.

Supervises: Housemen and Trainees.

Coordinates with: Housekeeping Control Desk, Laundry, Room Service, Engineering.

Summary Job: 1. Clean guest bathrooms and replenish supplies.

2. Clean guest bedroom and replenish supplies as per room checklist.

3. Report missing or broken hotel property to the Floor Supervisor.

4. Maintain a polite, dignified and helpful attitude towards the guests.

5. Attend daily briefings and give attendance.

6. Receive allocation of floor and rooms.

7. Replenish maid cart with guest supplies, detergents and linen.

8. Count soiled linen handed over to floor linen room.

9. Hand over lost and found articles to Supervisor.

10. Change the water glasses daily and fill the water flasks.

11. Make a physical check of rooms for preparing the Housekeeping Occupancy List.

12. Turn down beds in the evening and draw the curtains.

13. Check that all bulbs and switches are working, in case of defect or fuse, report the same to the Floor Supervisor.

14. Remove and dispose of refuse and rubbish in the assigned area.

15. Return keys to the Housekeeping Department before going off duty.

16. Ensure that Housemen polish guest shoes and assist the Bell Boys in carrying luggage when required.

17. Prepare room checklist.

CHAPTER -4

PLANNING WORK OF HOUSEKEEPING DEPARTMENT

DAILY ROUTINES AND SYSTEMS IN THE HOUSEKEEPING DEPARTMENT (HOUSEKEEPING SCHEDULE AND RECORDS)

At 7.00 or 8.00 a.m. when the staff come to work they must first punch- in their card to prove they are on duty at the timekeeper's office. Then they go to the locker room and change into their uniform and then report to work at the housekeeping office. (It is usual that they exchange their uniform, on a clean for dirty basis, the evening before and leave it clean and ready for use in their locker.) In this way, they do not waste time queuing for a clean uniform in the morning.

At the housekeeping office, the work is allocated and keys are distributed. Generally, the staff is made to sign for the keys they take after allocation of work. There is a register kept in the housekeeping office for recording the staff presence per section. Normally, one prepares the book according to the rota that day with a pencil. Then one ink in attendance as they arrive, this book is called the HOUSEKEEPING DAY BOOK.

Each morning reception sends information to the Housekeeping Office regarding the occupancy of the hotel and the anticipated checkouts for the day. Previously, one has received a forecast of occupancy. When a computer is in use all information comes through this. The aim is to cover the work according to the occupancy with the staff who present themselves for work.

If there is a shortage of staff, one has to divide the work to the staff present. We call this splitting section. People who have vacant rooms are first given the extra rooms, then the section with no checkouts, and then everybody is given an extra room or two, as necessary.

The ideally designed Housekeeping Office has a counter in front of which the assistant or supervisor present themselves and behind which the assistant or supervisor enters their name in the daybook and hands them the keys and they sign the key register. The keys are kept in a key box, which is lockable and on a wall near the counter. It has hooks numbered according to the floor and section for each key.

Cleaning Schedule

Month: _________   Year: _________

Day	Counter Tops	Cutting Boards (scrub first)	Meat Saw	Meat Slicer	Ice Machine	Food Equipment	Hand Sinks	Washrooms
	Wipe & Wash with Soap then Rinse with Bleach						Clean & Equip with Hand Soap & Single Use Towels	
1								
2								
3								
4								
5								
6								
7								
8								
9								
10								
11								
12								
13								
14								
15								
16								
17								
18								
19								
20								
21								
22								
23								
24								
25								
26								
27								
28								
29								
30								
31								

Normally each room attendant is given a worksheet with the rooms of the section printed on; vacant and anticipated check-outs are also noted on this. This helps them to know the situation in their section. The procedure usually is that the worksheet is on a clipboard with a pencil attached to it which is put on the trolley and the room attendants tick the rooms they have serviced so that the floor supervisor can see at a glance what work has been and has been not completed. Often, the same form is used for the maid's report card.

At the end of the day, keys and work cards have to be returned to the office. It is important that any room not serviced is noted down to be passed on to the evening shift for servicing.

At about 2.00 p.m. each afternoon, each floor supervisor does checking on the floors to see if there are any rooms still with DND notices or D/

L. She should then calls these rooms to see if they require service. The supervisor's part of the dialogue should be something like the following: 'Good afternoon Sir/Madam, this is the housekeeping supervisor speaking. Sorry to disturb you. What time would you like your room to be serviced today please?'

Room attendants are not allowed to telephone guests. If there is no reply on the phone, the Supervisor and room attendants proceed to the room.

Since hotels supply their staff with duty meals, nobody is allowed to go out of the premises until the end of their shift. This must be very clearly understood by all.

Staff is cautioned to immediately report any abnormalities to the housekeeping office, e.g., suspicious-looking people, abnormal noise or behaviour, people loitering in the corridors. In case of a room that should be Check out (C/O) that day; sometimes P/L - Packed luggage or N/P - Not packed is noted.

The floor supervisors collect all the reports from their maids and these are taken to the housekeeping office where the HOUSEKEEPING/ HOUSEKEEPER'S REPORT is made out. This is for the whole hotel and composed through the information given by each maid's report.

Maid's Report

Each room attendant prepares a report on the status of rooms allotted to him/her. Status means the letting situation of the room if it is a checkout, a stayover, or a vacant room, etc. This is a physical check of the status of rooms and all the reports are collected together to form one housekeeping report, which goes to Reception. It should tally with the reception records.

In case of discrepancies, the Reception notifies Housekeeping who has to re-check.

Reports are usually handed over every morning and afternoon. Some hotels do it at 9 p.m. but this is rare.

The possible status of rooms is as follows:

Checkout: C/O - means the guest has departed. The room is not

occupied.

Stay/Over: S/O - means the guest is staying on and not leaving

today. The room is occupied.

Vacant: V - means the room was not let.

Out-of-Order: O.O.O - means the room is under repair of some type.

(N. B. sometimes R is put beside check-out rooms to indicate that it is clean and ready to relet.)

An example of a MAID'S REPORT

The column for the no. of persons means the number of people occupying the room should be noted by the number of beds used or in a double-bedded room, by the indication of male and female clothes usually.

The column for comments is usually used to note a baby-cot or extra bed present in the room.

Since the room attendant cannot always enter the room, they make the following notes in the status column: -

D.N.D.: Do not disturb notice on the door.

D/L: The door is double locked.

OCC: The room is occupied but the room attendant cannot enter.

Lost and Found

The Housekeeping department in a hotel deals with all the lost and found property since most of it comes from the rooms. It is during checkout, room cleaning and inspection when it is found.

Articles lost in public areas such as bars, restaurants, lobby, cloakrooms are also given to the housekeeping office.

Whatever is found in staff areas such as canteen, locker room, and offices is also handed to housekeeping.

Sometimes articles are found in the linen, e.g., pyjamas accidentally collected in the sheets. The staff has to be cautioned about shaking out the sheets and towels so that this does not happen.

In the guests' laundry and dry-cleaning, it is important to check the pockets for any forgotten items; these are then immediately returned to the respective guests. It is surprising what can be left in pockets – money, passports, etc.

In the housekeeping office, a record of all the lost and found articles is kept, e.g., LOST AND FOUND REGISTER.

Each article is given a serial number, which makes it easy to locate in the storage. The best way of doing this is by numbers 1/1, 1/2 where 1 means January.

1/1 The first thing found in January. 1/2 The second thing found in January.

Therefore, 9/12 means the twelfth thing found in September.

The first number indicates the month, the second the serial number of the article.

Where found means room number usually or public area or location where found.

Article and description should be clear, e.g., shoes are not enough. Is it 1 shoe or a pair of shoes, ladies or gents, what colour or is it a pair of sandals.

Finder's name is important to record for possible distribution later.

Disposal must also be recorded, e.g., returned to guest or finder or even used by the hotel. Often hotels will use certain articles, e.g., swimsuits can be kept by the pool attendants in their cupboard for a loan to guests who forgot theirs.

On receipt of each article lost and found in the Housekeeping Office, it is recorded in the lost and found register, then packed in a clear plastic bag for easy identification. It is then stapled, closed and a tag is attached bearing the same information as in the lost and found register.

Usually, there is a small storage room for lost and found. This is divided into columns and the articles are stored there according to the serial number for easy location. (Sometimes, there is a lost and found cupboard in the housekeeping office to store the current week's articles, as the guest is likely to trace it.)

A file of lost and found queries is often also kept in hotels. Lost and found file usually records:

Most hotels keep articles for six months, but sometimes the law may require longer. (Usually, valuables are kept for one year).

In the cashier's office in a hotel, there are safe-deposit boxes where the guests can keep their valuables. Information about this is given in the rooms. A hotel then is not responsible if the guest loses his valuables because he left them in his room. Usually, the Executive Housekeeper has a safe deposit box to keep the housekeeping lost and found valuables. Since she is not on duty 24 hours a day, the key to this is deposited in a sealed signed envelope with the cashier and the duty manager can then at any time return the article to a guest. This must be signed in and out in the cashier's key register.

(One usually notes in a red pen in the lost and found register when an article is in the safety deposit box.)

Guests may phone, write or telex to inquire about their lost articles. They may ask the hotel to post them or give to someone on their behalf or they collect it themselves on a subsequent visit. Hotels do not charge for this postage. If the guest or someone else collects it personally, the hotel gets them to sign the tag attached to the article. Then these tags are filed. If it is posted, the Executive Housekeeper signs and notes down the details like the date posted on, name and address of the guest on the back of the tag and then it is filed. A compliment slip or a letter is enclosed with returned goods usually.

When the storage time is over, goods are returned to the finder. Then the Executive Housekeeper signs all the tags and this acts as a gate pass for the staff. It encourages honesty to return the goods to the finder. Some hotels organize sales of lost and found but this does not encourage the same honesty and staff feels the hotel is profiting from what could be given free to them.

Some hotels return valuables to the finder. Some sell them and put the money in with the tips to distribute to the whole department.

Each hotel has a slightly different policy on lost and found distribution.

Sometimes guests offer a reward to the finder of valuables and always the hotel lets the finder keep this for the honesty shown.

It is a good policy if a hotel can encourage the staff to phone the housekeeping office immediately when an article is found in a room. Then the desk clerk can ascertain from the front office if the guest has checked out of the hotel or not. Frequently, guests have left the room but their baggage can be in the luggage room still, then the article/s can be returned to the guest. This also gives a good impression to the guest of honesty and efficiency on the part of the hotel.

Perishables, e.g., food, flowers, etc., are not stored. They are given to the staff on a gate pass. Very dirty articles are discarded.

Checklists and Work Cards

Checklists are usually used in checking performance or work that has been completed. Thus, they are usually used by a supervisor.

Work cards are a list of tasks with instructions on how or when to do a job or jobs. The staff usually uses them.

Both checklists and work cards are, in fact, forms of reminder. They are usually printed and laminated with plastic.

One usually issues these to the new staff who have been newly recruited and trained.

Some hotels have checklists for spot-checking rooms in their properties to ensure correct standards are being maintained throughout their chain of hotels.

Handling Room Transfer/Changes

A guest may wish to transfer to another room for many reasons. They include:

Type of bed

Room too small

Room too expensive

Noise

Poor view

Colour/decor of the room

Faulty electrical equipment/s

Too far or near to the elevator, etc.

In such cases, the request is generally accepted, subject to availability. The Front Office Department informs Housekeeping to change the guest's room. The Front Office Department informs all the relevant departments accordingly.

Types of Shift

1.   **Straight shift:** Staff work a specific number of hours continually depending on whether they are full time, part-time or casual, on permanent days, afternoon or night.

2.   **Split shift:** They are still quite common in the areas of cleaning. Housekeeping department staff work a specified number of hours during the peak period, then have a few hours of rest and return to cover the next peak period.

In all, they may not work more than 8 hours but a shift may cover 12 hours during the day.

3.   **Rotating shift:** Another of the staff will usually cover a work period of 24 hours 7 days per week for 52 weeks of the year. Three shifts of 8 hours rotation in a pre-arranged manner, e.g., 6 am to 2 pm, 2 pm to 10 pm and 10 pm to 6 am. They may have 4 days of work and 2 days off. Then they move into the next shift, and so on. The length of shift or cycle will depend on the number of staff, the average working hours per week or fortnight and the number of working days in rotation to off duty periods.

4.   **Alternating shift:** Staff work, either a specified number of early or late shifts each week or once a week. An early shift followed by one week on a late shift.

HOTEL MAINTENANCE

Definition: Maintenance is defined as the activity by which the equipment is kept in the same condition as when they were purchased.

TYPES OF MAINTENANCE

Maintenance is of four types:

1. Routine/planned maintenance

2. Preventive maintenance

3. Breakdown/emergency maintenance

4. Reporting maintenance

1. Routine/planned maintenance

It is a detailed look at all the points of equipment. It is done regularly; the checking time depends on the following points:

(a) The use of the equipment

(b) The nature of the equipment

(c) Legal requirement

2. Preventive maintenance

It is the maintenance in which equipment is prevented from being broken down. The housekeeper or supervisor is responsible for daily checking of the equipment to find out any fault/mistake. The purpose of preventive

maintenance is to prevent the misuse of the machines and to see that the equipment is working properly.

3. Breakdown/emergency maintenance

The maintenance where equipment is brought when it has broken down. This is an emergency service given by the maintenance department for which every hotel has a provision. The objective of breakdown maintenance is to repair the equipment. Many hotels maintain a stock of equipment (parts) to avoid problems arising due to the breakdown of equipment.

4. Reporting maintenance

This is a type of maintenance where the staff of a department has to check the equipment they use. In case they find that the equipment is not working properly, they should inform their supervisor, who then reports to the maintenance department. The maintenance staff has to check and detect the fault /mistake in the equipment. There are two types of mistake:

(a) Major mistake

(b) Minor mistake

(a)　　　　MAJOR MISTAKE: The major mistakes are always reported to the top management, as the correction of such mistakes is not within the capacity of the supervisor.

(b)　　　　MINOR MISTAKE: Is reported to the supervisor and is corrected at once.

OBJECTIVES OF THE MAINTENANCE DEPARTMENT

1. Enhance the life of machine or equipment

2. Aim at maximum efficiency

3. Enhance cost-effectiveness

4. Ensure user or operator's satisfaction

5. Ensure user or operator's safety

6. Provide trouble-free service

7. Contribute to the smooth functioning of other departments

8. Provide coordination between departments

SIGNIFICANCE OF MAINTENANCE DEPARTMENT

Since, the hotel uses many different kinds of manual, electrical and electronic equipment, it is imperative to have a full-fledged and functional maintenance department.

This department ensures that proper and timely maintenance of the various equipment is carried out not only to increase the life of the equipment but also to use it properly for the purpose for which it was purchased. The maintenance department works in close coordination with the Housekeeping department.

GOOD LIGHTING

Good lighting should be in harmony with the function of the area for which it is intended. The basic purpose of lighting is to eliminate darkness as well as to light up the area in the most decorative, practical and efficient way.

It is a well-known fact that without light, there is no colour and hence, its importance. In the darkness no colour is visible but we can feel the texture, so visual significance is not there unless there is a source of light. As light rays strike a surface, they are either absorbed or reflected. The colour and texture of the substance depends upon the light rays that fall on them and further shows the reflective quality.

Lighting is given a lot of importance by the hotelier, decorator and engineer mainly because the light is a science which has to be blended with the beauty of the building/structure. Lighting fixtures and their placement are developed after taking their aesthetic as well as functional aspect into consideration.

The most significant problem in the design of any lighting system lies in understanding what good lighting is.

Good lighting design is realized if:

A. All spaces (entry, work area, public area, exit, etc.) are composed properly in a clear hierarchy of importance and purpose.

B. Makes it possible to see quickly without strain.

C. The lighting mood is consistent with the function and design of each space and is also pleasing to the eye.

D. It promotes productivity.

E. Eliminates hazards.

F. It is readily maintainable.

G. It is energy saving.

H. It has fully utilized the potential of daylight when it is available.

DEFINITION OF LIGHT

LIGHT IS A FORM OF ENERGY THAT ENABLES THE EYE TO SEE. It can be the natural light of the sun or the artificial light of lamps. Light levels are measured in **lux** and **lumen**.

The amount of light given out by light is measured in lumen. However, some of this light is lost as it gets absorbed by mist, dirty fittings, coloured shades, dark coloured furnishings and by distance. All these features determine the amount of light which reaches the surface.

Therefore, a lumen is a unit for measuring the source and quality of light emitted from the source and lux is the unit measuring the amount of light, which reaches the surface.

TYPES OF LIGHTING

Lighting is of four types:

(a) Direct lighting

(b) Indirect lighting

(c) Semi-direct lighting

(d) Diffused lighting

(a)　　　**Direct lighting:** Direct lighting is where the light is directed straight from the bulb into the room. It is the type that is produced by the most table and floor lamps. It is the light which shines directly on a limited area.

(b)　　　**Indirect lighting:** It is where all the light is directed on to the ceiling or wall from which it is reflected into the room.

(c)　　　**Semi-direct lighting:** It is where some of the light is directed into the room and some are allowed to be directed and reflected from the ceiling.

(d)　　　**Diffused lighting:** It is where the bulb or the light source is completely enclosed and the light is diffused through a translucent shade or material. Curtains, wall or ceiling panels can conceal the light source.

CHAPTER- 5

HOTEL GUEST ROOM

<u>TYPES OF ROOM</u>

Each hotel has a variety of rooms according to the needs of the guest which are divided into two types.

Common or conventional rooms Uncommon/special types of rooms

Common/Conventional Types of Rooms

1.   **Single room:** The term refers to a room with a standard single bed to provide sleeping accommodation to one person. The room furnishing and fixtures, as well as amenities and facilities standards, would depend upon the standard of the hotel. The size of a single bed is generally 6' × 3'.

2.   **Double room:** Double room term refers to a room which has a double bed and provides sleeping comforts for two persons. A double bed is a large bed. The size of a double bed is generally 6' × 6'.

3.   **Twin-bedded room:** Twin-bedded room is a room with two identical twin beds separated by a small bedside table. This room provides sleeping accommodation for two persons.

4.   **Suite:** The term suite refers to a set of two rooms out of which one is a bedroom and the other is a sitting room or living room. Forgoing from one room to another the use of corridor is not required. The suite is a costly room in a hotel. There are various types of suites such as:

(a)   **Single suite:** It is a single room with a sitting room attached to it and meant for one person's sleeping comfort.

Uncommon/Special Types of Rooms

1.   **Lanai -** It is a room with a good view; generally situated at the corners of the building with a good view of the surrounding area like hills or mountains, lakes or seas, gardens or forests or any other natural beauty. It may be double, twin or suite.

2.   **Hollywood twin room -** It is a twin-bedded room with a common headboard, which is attached to the wall and not to the beds. The headboard should be well decorated with carvings or covered by any furniture covering with stuffing.

3.   **Utility room/Efficiency room -** This room is generally found with a family room. It is a room with kitchen facility

4.   **Cabana -** This room is situated beside the swimming pool and is used to change clothes. It must have a locker facility and a bathroom with a shower.

5.   **Studio room -** It is a room with a bed that can be turned into a sofa when not in use.

6.   **Parlour -** It is a sitting room. It may or may not have a bed facility.

7.   **Murphy room -** A room with a bed that can be set up against the wall when not in use. It may not have a picture frame or headboard at the back of the bed.

8.   **Hospitality room -** It is a room which is used only by the residential guests to entertain their guests and to hold parties or meetings. It is charged on an hourly basis.

9.	**Family room** - A room with a king-sized bed or two double beds enough to fit a family of four members.

10.	**Interconnecting room** - Two rooms connected by a door known as interconnecting rooms. The door can be shut to make it two rooms.

11.	**Penthouse suite** - It is the suite part which is open to the sky. The open part is covered with glass. It is generally situated on the top floor of a hotel.

12.	**Duplex room** - It is a suite situated on two different levels and is connected by a staircase. The bedroom is on the upper level and the sitting room is on the lower level.

13.	**Presidential suite** - It is a suite with two or more bedrooms, each one having attached bathrooms.

14.	**Junior suite** - In a large room, partition done by using a wooden board is known as Junior suite.

EACH ROOM MAY CONTAIN

• A single/queen-sized bed - This may be called a single room.

• Two single beds - This may be called a twin room.

• Three single beds or a single and double bed - This may be called a triple room.

• There may also be standard, 'Executive' or deluxe rooms.

• The term 'suite' usually means that in addition to the bedroom, it may have an adjoining sitting room.

TYPES OF HOTEL ROOMS AND VARIOUS TYPES OF BEDS

Hotel rooms always have attached bathroom facilities these days. Hotels can offer single, twin or double rooms. That means a single room is a room with a bed for one person.

A twin room is a room with two single beds. A double room is a room with one bed for a couple.

Some hotels do not build any single room as one can always stay in a twin or double room. Some hotels use only twins rooms, as it is possible to make a double bed by crossing mattresses.

There are hotels which put two double beds in each room so that they can be used in single, twin or family rooms.

Usually, hotels allow a family to have a small extra bed for a child or a baby cot or a crib for a baby in the same room where the parents are residing. Some hotels do not charge extra for this but start to charge if the child is over a set age, e.g., 10 years or if there is an extra bed for an adult. Hotels charge different rates for a single or double occupancy of a room. There are also beds called queen-size and king-size. This idea originated from the USA, and it means large-double beds and some hotels use these in their suites.

A suite is a set of rooms and they interconnect, of which at least one room is not a bedroom, e.g., one can have a suite of a bedroom (single, double or twin) and bathroom and sitting room.

Sometimes, the sitting room also has a full bathroom, (so if there are two people, they each have a bathroom). Sometimes, the sitting room has only cloakroom facilities or can have a tiny kitchenette. Many hotels have a sitting room with connecting doors on one side to a twin-bedded room. Since these connecting doors can be locked and unlocked, it enables the suite to offer twin or double facilities. Of course one can also open all the doors to form a two-bedroom suite.

Sometimes, hotel sitting rooms do not have dining tables as the room service departments have trolleys that open as tables. However, more elaborate suites can have a separate dining room, a study and a kitchen and sometimes a bar can be included in the sitting room, then the sitting room needs to be very large and, of course, one or two bedrooms are included in such a suite. Some sitting rooms have a dining alcove or a dining area. Suites, of course, cost much more than a room in a hotel.

There are two other types of room which offer sitting facilities. One type is a large-sized bedroom with a sitting area provided with chairs and usually a sofa and a coffee table. This is a combination of bedroom/sitting room. Hotels give various names to such rooms as the executive room.

The other type is a studio room which is a room using a bed that either converts into a sofa or pulls out of a cupboard thus making the room like a sitting room by day and a bedroom by night. The sofa type bed, as well as the wall cupboard bed, can be a single or a double room. Studio rooms are very useful for businessmen as they can use their rooms like an office by day. Most hotels do not charge more for a studio room but generally charge more for the bedroom/ sitting room combination type, as it is usually larger than an ordinary room.

VIP ROOMS

VIP means a very important person and while all guests are important to a hotel, some are selected for special care and attention.

Most hotels have categories of VIPs, e.g., VIP I, VIP II, VIP III and VIP IV.

Heads of state, ministers, very famous personalities and international celebrities.

Full Bar—

Whisky, Gin, Vodka, Aperitif, Soft Drinks, Mixers, Water, Nuts, Cocktail, Biscuits and Beer.

Large Flower Set – Up (1 per room) Large Fruit Basket –

Chocolates, Petit Fours Other Items

Bathrobes, Towelling Slippers, Third Sheet, Bath Foam, Eau- De-Cologne, Comb, Disposable Toothbrush and Paste.

It is quite costly to offer all these things so VIP I is only for a few select people.

Presidents of large companies, top people in a hotel's company, ambassadors, well-known personalities and other such officials. Partial Bar—

Beer, Soft Drinks, Bottled water. Medium-sized Flower Set-Up Medium-sized Fruit Basket – Chocolates, Petit Fours

Other Items

Bathrobes, Towelling Slippers, Third Sheet, Bath Foam, Eau- De- Cologne, Comb, Disposable Toothbrush and Paste.

Regular guests, crew members and people are known to the hotel. Bottled Water.

Small Flower Set-Up Small Fruit Basket

Other Items

Bathrobes, Towelling Slippers, Third Sheet, Bath Foam, Eau- De-Cologne, Comb, Disposable Toothbrush and Paste.

Group leaders, Tour leaders, journalists. Bottled Water.

Small Flower Set-Up Small Fruit Basket.

Extra Facilities Given To VIPs

VIPs along with getting these extra facilities also get a very carefully checked room. Usually assistant or Executive Housekeeper does this checking. They get the best treatment possible.

It must be remembered that the giveaways for VIPs vary from company to company and even from hotel to hotel.

Some hotels even give a small basket of fruit to all arrivals, which is a very nice gesture. Some hotels supply chocolates or cookies along with fruit basket.

The Housekeeping department is informed daily from Reception about VIP arrivals and VIPs already in the house. One tries to get VIP rooms ready as early as possible.

Some hotels give little gifts to their VIPs. Some give personalized notepaper and matches. Many hotels give larger and different soap to VIPs and some give a soap basket. Many hotels put a bud vase with one rose in each room.

GUEST'S SPECIAL REQUIREMENT

Apart from all the normal facilities and supplies provided in the rooms in hotels, sometimes guests request extra or additional items. Usually, they telephone to the housekeeping office for their requests.

An extra blanket, pillow or towels are very normal requests. One sometimes gets a guest asking for a bathrobe. (Most hotels supply bathrobe only to VIP guests). Sometimes, guests may ask for additional supplies, e.g., more shampoo, etc.

Not all requests by guests are for additional or extra items, some are for service, e.g., the room to be serviced or shoe cleaning or a sewing or mending job to be done.

Hotels stock certain items, which they loan to guests, e.g., electric shaver and hairdryer. These items have to be noted in the housekeeping office and collected again, usually the same day to ensure they are not lost. In some hotels, they also loan heated hair curlers for ladies.

Since many hotel guests are businessmen, so one gets requests for scissors, a few sheets of plain paper and other such items.

Occasionally, one gets requests for an item like extra furniture, e.g., a desk lamp, an extra chair or two, a card table.

Some guests who suffer from backache require a bed board, which is a piece of wood placed under the mattress to make it firm. Also, some guests are allergic to feather pillows and ask for foam ones.

Equipment for babies such as potty, baby bath, cot, high chair and heating food plate are frequent requests.

Extra beds (which usually folds) and are known as ROLLAWAY are a necessary item required on demand. (Since many hotels charge for extra beds, housekeeping must always notify Reception if the guest approached housekeeping directly).

Some guests require floral displays.

Guests sometimes request an electric trouser press.

DO NOT DISTURB ROOMS

Procedures should be set up for dealing with rooms that have **Do Not Disturb** signs after 2.30 p.m. to 3 p.m. Room attendants should point these out to their supervisors. The supervisors in turn usually ask the rooms division to check these rooms by phone or in person. In most cases, room attendants should not knock on a door with a **Do Not Disturb** sign or enter the room. If the property's policy allows room attendants to knock on doors with **Do Not Disturb** signs afternoon or 1 p.m. The room attendants should be instructed to follow the usual procedures for entering the guest room. If the guest is in the room, the room attendant should ask politely when the room could be serviced.

ROOM LAYOUT AND STANDARD CONTENTS OF A GUEST ROOM IN A FIVE STAR HOTEL

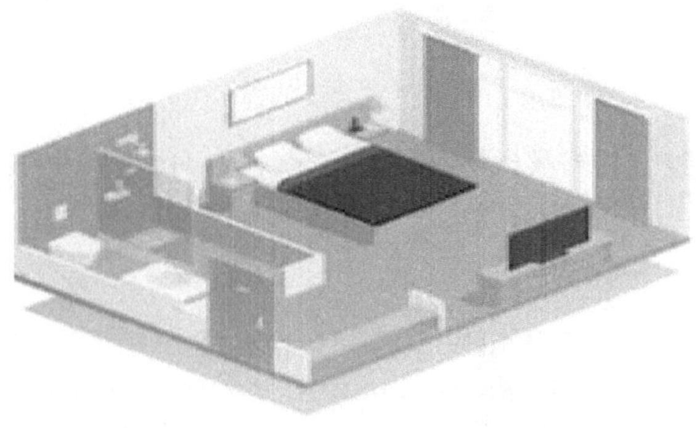

Standard contents of a guest room in a five-star hotel

1. BED:

Mattress 6" thick

Mattress protector - 1

Bedsheets - 2

Blanket - 1

Night sheet - 1

Pillows - 2

Pillowcases - 2

Pillowslip - 2

Bed cover - 1

2. BEDSIDE TABLE:

Telephone

Inter-departmental telephone book/directory Telephone pad with pencil

Bedside table lamps Ashtray with matchbox One Bible and Geeta Vacuum flask on a tray

Sterilized glasses - 2

3.   **SEATING ARRANGEMENT:** Sofas or easy chairs - 2 Column lamp – 1

4.   **COFFEE TABLE:** Daily newspaper Ashtray with matchbox

Periodicals and hotel magazine

5.   **SOFT FURNISHINGS:** Heavy curtains/Draperies Sheer curtains

Venetian blinds Cushion covers

6.   **DRESSING CUM WRITING TABLE:** Mirror with wall mounted lamps on either side Writing folder containing

Letterheads Envelopes Aerogrammes Picture postcards

House rules and regulations card Mail forwarding address slip Expecting a calling card

Pen and pencil Restaurant menu card Rail and airtime tables

7.   **ALSO ON THE TABLE:** Room service menu card Suggestion folder

Ashtray with matchbox Candlestand

Hotel's sales promotion brochures

8.   **IN THE DRAWER:** Breakfast doorknob card Dutch wife (sewing kit) Fax/Telex forms

a.   ON THE FLOOR:
     Waste paper basket near writing table

b.   . ENTRANCE DOORKNOB:
     'Do Not Disturb' Card

     'Please Clean My Room' Card Fire exit map

c.   . FLOOR COVERING:

Wall-to-Wall carpet

d. IN THE CLOSET OR WARDROBEL- laundry bags Valet bags Dry-cleaning slips Laundry slips
Please collect my laundry' Card

9. OTHER ITEMS:

Luggage racks TV set Refrigerator

10. **BATHROOM:** Bathtub Bathmat

Bath soap Shampoo sachet

11. **BATH TOWEL RACK:** Turkish bath towels - 2 Curtain rod

Shower curtain

12. **WASHBASIN COUNTER**:

Mirror mounted on wall Hand towels - 2

Face towels - 2 Tooth/Gargle glasses - 2 Shower cap

Face tissue box Hand soap Freshen up packet Ashtray

Extra toilet roll Soapsuds

13. **UNDER THE COUNTER**:

Waste paper basket

14. **WATER CLOSET:** Sanitary disinfectant band Sanitary basket

Sanitary bag Toilet roll Toilet paper Odonil stick Shoeshine strip Wall telephone

15. BATHROOM DOOR:

Full-length mirror

Peg hooks – at the back of the door Bottle opener – at the side of the door

FURNISHINGS, FIXTURES AND EQUIPMENT

Furnishings, fixtures, and equipment is a broad category which includes everything from the grand piano used in the ballroom and the finest furnishings in the presidential suite to the ceiling and plumbing fixtures and the ash urns. Furniture usually is broken down into the following categories like **case goods,** which can be anything with a top and sides, like dressers, armoires and desks; softgoods, like as fabrics and bed covers; seating, like sofas, chairs, bar stools and decorative benches; tables, from accent or occasional tables to restaurant and function tables; and lighting and accessories, including artwork and plants.

Selecting Furnishings, Fixtures and Equipment

Furnishings and fixtures help in defining the image of the hotel. Key factors considered in furniture selection include:

Appearance

Availability

Comfort

Function

Guarantees and/or the integrity of the manufacturer or vendor

Cost

Repairability

Durability

Appearance

The most subjective of all criteria, appearance is still important. There are so many styles, there are certain rules for choosing design elements:

1. Large patterns exist in large rooms; small patterns in small areas. Complementary patterns can be mixed, if they harmonize in terms of style and colour.

2. Room look bigger in light colours and smaller in bright colours. Sometimes this rule is broken above to make a small restaurant look even more elegant and secluded.

3. Avoid clashing colours.

Appearance should be weighed against the look of the property's architecture, the size of its space, and its geographic setting. Furnishings should blend with the wall coverings, floor coverings, and architectural elements rather than drawing attention to themselves—unless they are meant to make a strong statement.

Availability

Availability is an important subject, especially when opening a hotel. The interior designer notifies department heads on the pre-opening team when the furniture fixtures and equipment (FF&E) will be delivered. Availability for every product, no matter how small, should be checked. Late arrival can postpone the opening and hurt the hotel's image.Replacement is another consideration. Although properties generally stock a certain number of replacement pieces for furnishings, they cannot afford to carry a replacement for the entire inventory of furnishings. The executive housekeeper should determine how long it will take to get replacement pieces; how long replacement pieces will be available to the company (many styles eventually go out of stock); and what provisions will be made for matching dye lots or wood tones.

Comfort

Comfort is paramount for guestroom chairs, chairs used in auditoriums, meeting rooms, and fine dining restaurants where it is desirable to have patrons linger. **Ergonomic chairs,** provide both full back support and, frequently, a height adjustment, are now becoming standard as desk chairs in business-oriented properties, from the deluxe range down to economy hotels. However, in outlets where high customer turnover is the goal, seating is usually less comfortable. Stackable chairs used for banquets and large conventions fall somewhere between the two extremes.

Climate also affects comfort. Breathable fabrics, like as cotton or cotton blends, are better choices than vinyl or moulded plastic for warmer climates. Also, fabrics must be soft. At times, in the search for durability, the fabric selected is durable but too stiff or rough to be comfortable.

Contract seating may range from below $30 for a utility dining chair or folding chair, to several hundred dollars for custom chairs upholstered with premium fabrics. Cost means more than the initial capital outlay. To figure out the true cost, other factors must be considered:

• Cost of regular maintenance

• Cost and projected frequency of repairs

• Cost of deep cleaning

• The average life expectancy of the piece

The cost will also be influenced by how much repair can be done on the property. Another consideration is how often the piece can be refinished, reworked or reupholstered.

Function

The function for which a place is planned influences the choice of FF&E. The primary considerations when making the determination include whether the furniture is suitable for the function of the room and whether it will wear well under these conditions.

Other factors also affect function, for example, a chair with **wall-saver legs**— legs that splay out to the back so that the chair hits the baseboard before hitting the wall— take up extra space but save on maintenance and repair costs for the walls. Coasters or rollers may be desirable on chairs in a dining room with deep pile carpet. Ease of maintenance is another aspect of function.

Guarantees and/or the Integrity of the Source

This consideration is particularly important for the executive housekeeper, who will have to invoke the guarantee of any design element that fails to live up to the manufacturer's claims. Well-made furniture has a guarantee or warranty. If any piece does not exist, the dealer or vendor usually will pick it up, replace it and then settle the matter with the manufacturer. Due to the volume of furniture purchased by a hotel, finding a defective item is common.

Fabrics are mainly guaranteed by their manufacturer rather than the furniture manufacturer. Each item should be checked for its warranty or guarantee, and this paperwork should be kept on file. Date of delivery should be written on each item's record.

If an item is easier to repair the longer it will last and the more cost-effective it will be. Wood is among the easiest materials to repair. Often, a stain stick to touch up dents and scratches will delay complete refinishing. Even complete refinishing is not an overwhelming task.

Durability

Deluxe hotels can have solid wood furniture. Most hotels have furniture which combines wood with plastic or laminate. Laminates made to look like wood are far more durable because they can withstand wetness and stains and simply be wiped clean. In future, most mid-tier and economy hotel chains would be moving more and more towards nonwood furnishings.

It is not only the material but the construction that affects longevity. Hardwood chairs would have joints which are both glued and screwed together. Connecting rods, called **stretchers,** must join all legs together except at the front of the chair. Rear legs of wood chairs must be steam-bent with the wood grain, rather than cut from cross-grain pieces that can split easily.

Generally, softgoods like the bedspreads, sheers, and pillow shams, etc., are replaced every three to five years. Casegoods are expected to last for 10 to 20 years. Upscale hotels renovate more frequently than midtier' or economy hotels. Upscale rooms can be renovated every five to seven years; a fullscale, property-wide renovation may be undertaken for every 10 to 15 years.

<u>GUEST SUPPLIES</u>

Linen supply

Bedspread/night spread

Bedsheet

Pillowcases

Bath towel

Face towel

Hand towel

Bath mat

Mattress protector (optional)

Room Supply

Water tumbler

Water jug

Ashtrays

Matchboxes

Candle stand with candle

Sewing kit

Plastic sheet bags (laundry bag)

Laundry list

Room Stationery

Guest stationery (pad, letterhead, envelopes)

Telegraph/fax form

Ballpoint pen

Laundry form

Guest comment card

Service directory

Breakfast Knob Card

'Polish My Shoe' Card

'Do Not Disturb' Card/'Clean My Room' Card

Guesthouse rules

Important telephone number list

Bath Room Supplies

Water tumbler

Soapdish with soap

Candle stand with candle

Ashtray with matchbox

Toilet tissue rolls

Shower cap

Shampoo bottle

Shoeshine strip

Blade dispenser

Disposable bag

GUEST AMENITIES

This is an important activity in which a list of amenities to be prepared and sent to all departments such as food and beverage, pantry, room service and housekeeping, and so on so that they can make necessary and appropriate arrangement in advance.

Depending upon the status of the guest several amenities can be provided in the room and bathroom, such as fruits, flowers, pastries, cookies, pralines, cake, champagne bottle, mini-bar complimentary, dry fruits, cigarettes and cigars, personalized stationery, bathrobe, weighing scale, moisturizer, soaps, talcum powder, toothpaste, toothbrush and shaving kit, and so on.

CORRIDORS

The corridors should be wide enough to enable the use of wheelchairs and trolleys, for people to pass comfortably and to prevent any feeling of claustrophobia. Steps can prove a great inconvenience for the use of wheelchairs and trolleys and where possible they should be replaced by ramps.

Many corridors have little or no external light, and to prevent accidents, adequate artificial lighting is necessary throughout the 24 hours. Guests can then see their way clearly and the room numbers easily. In some buildings, during the day, borrowed light is provided on the corridors by having fanlights over the doors but, when this is the case, guests can be disturbed at night by the corridor lights. To conform with local by-laws, secondary lighting must be available in hotels to show up emergency exists. With modern methods of construction, there are not much fire risks in a new building, but under the Fire Precautions Act, 1971 fire doors or fire breaks are necessary to confine a fire to one part of the building and to exclude draughts which might help spread the fire.

-

FLOOR PANTRIES

Each guest floor must have a floor pantry to keep a supply of linen, guest supplies and cleaning supplies for the floor. It is the housekeeping nerve centre for the floor. The floor pantry should keep one complete set of linen for that floor over and above what is in circulation in the rooms. The pantry should be away from guest view and situated at the service landing near the service elevators.

CHAPTER-6

CLEANING SCIENCE

PRINCIPLES OF CLEANING

Definition

The word 'clean' means something free from dust, dirt, stains, cobwebs, grease and other unwanted substances.

Why Clean?

To improve appearance, preserve the life of building/fabrics and to prevent infection.

How to Clean?

Dirt and dust are removed by:

n Washing, e.g., water and a cleaning agent

n Use hot and clean water, clean cloth and mops, clean bucket, mugs, correct cleaning agent, correct materials, appropriate technique and equipment, only freshly prepared solution/ disinfectant after cleaning

n Friction using an abrasive

n Static electricity (using a static mop sweeper)

n Suction using a vacuum cleaner

n Force, using pressurized water

n Sweep before you dust

n Allow time for the dust to settle (e.g., bed making) before dusting

Damp dusting is more effective than dry dusting, as it prevents dust from flying out

The damp duster must be washed well; otherwise, it leaves streak marks.

Give a final visual check after cleaning

Remember, cleanliness is important, hygiene is essential and professionalism is vital.

REASONS FOR CLEANING

To prevent the spread of infection and disease

To control the amount of dust in an area

To lengthen the life of the building, along with its various furniture, fixture and equipment (FE&E)

To provide a socially acceptable environment for the guests and staff of the hotel

To meet the requirements of health and safety of the inhabitants of the hotel

The Standards of Cleaning

This depends on the type of establishment and the various activities carried out in it. The standards are achieved by:

1. Selecting the correct method of cleaning

2. Carrying out the cleaning task at regular intervals

3. Effective quality control

4. Effective human resource (manpower) planning

The cleaning method, material and equipment required depends upon the following:

1. User (guest) requirements

2. The usage of the building

3. The type of surface and its physical and chemical properties

4. The nature of soiling

5. The degree of soiling

6. Traffic (people and equipment) in the area

7. The safety aspect of the staff engaged in cleaning

Nothing sends a stronger message than cleanliness in a hospitality operation, thus, cleaning is very important.

CLEANING TECHNIQUES (HOW TO CLEAN)

Dirt and dust are removed by:

Washing, e.g., water and a cleaning agent

Friction using an abrasive

Static electricity (using a static mop/sweeper)

Suction using a vacuum cleaner or wet pick up machine

Force using pressurized water

The exact method chosen depends on the type and amount of dirt and the surface to be cleaned.

Using the correct techniques is important, e.g., there is no point in dusting a deeply ingrained stain or wiping the bath when friction is required to clean it.

WATER AND CLEANING AGENTS

Water

Water is a cleaning agent but on its own, it does not 'wet' the surface properly.

By adding a chemical cleaning agent, cleaning is more effective.

Detergents

These are cleaning agents which, when used in conjunction with water, can loosen and remove dirt, and then hold it in suspension so that the dirt is not redeposited on the clean surface.

The three basic properties of detergents are:

1. Good wetting power

2. Good emulsifying power

3. Good suspension power

Detergents may be soapy or soapless or synthetic detergent.

The basic ingredients of any detergent are surface-active agents (or surfactants) which are the wetting agents that lower the surface tension of water and also emulsify the grease and suspend the soiling.

Surfactants are classified on the basis that when dissolved in water, some dissociate into positively or negatively charged ions, i.e., Cationic (+ve), Anionic (-ve) or non-ionic (neutral). Out of these, the non-ionic types of surfactants are most effective.

Other substances which are added to the detergents are alkaline builders, sodium sulphate, sodium carbonate, Hexa methylcellulose, ethyl hydroxy, ethylcellulose, sodium perborate, enzymes, germicides, perfumes or dyestuffs.

An ideal detergent has the following properties

Good wetting powers so that the solution penetrates between the article and the dirt particles

Good emulsifying power so that grease and oil are broken up and to some extent dissolved

Good suspending power so that the dirt particles are suspended in the solution and are readily soluble in water

Be effective in all types of water and should produce no scum or precipitation

Be effective over a wide range of surfaces

Be harmless to the articles and skin that it comes in contact with

Cleanse reasonably quickly and with minimum agitation

The various additives (chemical) that are added to both soaps and detergents to improve their performance are:

Washing soda (sodium carbonate)

Bleach (sodium perborate)

Fluorescent whiteners (liquid blue)

Perfumes and fragrances

Ground pumice powder (abrasives)

GENERAL CRITERIA FOR SELECTION OF CLEANING AGENTS

Strong agents not to be used

Check the sample before ordering

Good quality and a reputed product must be preferred

Always check the result of the cleaning agent and then use it

The cost factor should be seen before the selection

Compare the existing product with other products available in the market for competitive bargains and to have a better view of the availability of cleaning agents.

If possible, buy eco-friendly cleaning agents.

CLASSIFICATION OF CLEANING AGENTS

1.   **Neutral detergents:** Common/general purpose detergents used for washing dishes, damp dusting and mopping and routine cleaning tasks.

2.   **Alkali detergent:** These are corrosive and, thus, used for heavy tasks like stripping floors. These should not be used too often as they can damage surfaces. Some contain abrasives and should not be used on surfaces like plastic baths.

3.   **Acid cleaners:** Used for cleaning toilets and removing stains from baths and washbasins. It is important to follow the instruction carefully— never mix with other cleaning agents as the combination may produce harmful chemicals.

 These varies in strength from dilute (acetic acid) to strong (hydrochloric acid).

 These should always be used in a solution form, followed by thorough rinsing.

 Strong acids are highly corrosive and poisonous.

 Commonly used acids for cleaning purposes are citric, acetic, HCl, sodium sulphate, oxalic acid, etc.

4. **Solvent-based cleaners:** Can dissolve heavy deposits of grease and oil. Used for removing wax from wooden floors, for dry-cleaning and stain removal.

Solvents as Cleaning Agents

These chemicals are used for dry-cleaning and stain removal.

As they have a strong odour, they should be used in a well-ventilated room.

They evaporate easily and should be stored in airtight containers.

Most of them are highly inflammable and, thus, are to be used with caution.

As they are volatile, their fumes must not be allowed to mix.

They must be stored in well-labelled bottles/containers.

Because of their strong nature, they should be used in small amounts.

Some examples of solvents are:

Per chloro ethylene (dry-cleaning chemical)

Trichloroethylene

Methylated spirit

Turpentine oil (Thinner)

Carbon tetrachloride (CCl4)

Acetone

White petrol/spirit

Amyl acetate

5.	**Abrasive cleaners:** Scouring cleaners in powder, paste, cream or liquid form. Used for cleaning enamel and ceramic sanitary ware.

6. Alkaline cleaners:

These cleaners are good at removing greasy stains

n They are also used to neutralize the action of strong acid cleaners

 As some alkaline cleaners are strong, they should be carefully used, with the protection of rubber gloves

n Some examples of alkaline cleaners are

q Sodium bicarbonate (baking soda) (ph value 8)

q Sodium carbonate (washing soda) (ph value 10)

q Sodium hydroxide (caustic soda) (ph value14)

q Liquid ammonia (ph value 11)

q Hydrogen peroxide (ph value 10)

q Sodium perborate (bleaching powder) (ph value 10)

DISINFECTANT

The purpose of a disinfectant is to kill harmful bacteria. We can do this by:

1. **Heat:** This is the best and most effective method. However, not every surface can be cleaned in this way.

2. **Cleaning:** Thorough cleaning is the most effective way of removing bacteria, as where you have no dirt (visible or not visible), you will have no bacteria.

3. **Chemically:** Many people think using Dettol is the only way to clean chemically. However, chemical disinfectant is not usually necessary. In certain circumstances, it may be required after someone has got sick on a surface or another contamination has occurred. Chemical disinfectants should only be used after cleaning.

POINTS TO NOTE

1. Some chemical disinfectants are inactivated by Dirt &
Plastics

  The addition of other agents.

2. Follow instructions carefully by using the correct
dilution ratio.

3. All disinfectants take time to work.

POLISH

 Polishes are applied to a surface to form a protective
layer and guard against marks, stains and scratches.

 They also give a shiny appearance on a hard surface like
metal, furniture and floor.

 Before applying any polish, the surface that has to be
polished should be cleaned well and a thin layer of
polish should be applied.

 The surface should be rubbed with a soft cloth to get a
shiny finish.

 Too much polish creates a sticky surface which does not
look pleasing to the eye.

 Furniture polishes could be in paste, cream or liquid
form. They could be spirit-based or water-based.

 High-speed emulsion polishes are used in conjunction
with floor polishing machines or floor scrubbers.

 Before applying any polish, the previously applied
polish should be removed from the surface to be
polished.

FLOOR SEALS

 These are protective finishes which when applied on a
floor, forms a skin of plastic on it and thus protect the
floor.

Floor seals remain for several months on the floor and are durable and soil-resistant.

The various functions of floor seals are:

n To increase the life of a floor by eliminating direct wears

n Prevent entry of dirt or soil into a floor

n Protect the floor from chemicals

n Improve the appearance of a floor

n Reduce the cost of routine maintenance of the floor.

Various types of floor seals can be classified according to their main chemical component.

(a)   OLEO RESINOUS - This seal is made from oils, resins and thinner or any other organic solvent. It takes a long time to dry. Other types are one-pot plastic seal and two pot plastic seal. These

are used on wooden floors.

(b)   PIGMENTED SEAL- They give a better appearance to a floor, can be used on concrete floors also.

(c)   WATER-BASED SEALS- Consists of acrylic or other material dispersed in water. Easy-to-use, relatively cheap, can be used on various floors except for wood.

To remove the floor seal, special chemicals called 'stripper' are used.

USE, CARE AND STORAGE

1. Use of a cleaning agent should be done on a minimum basis as it spoils our environment. The amount used should be such that the cleaning task is not affected and the standards are maintained.

2. Care of a cleaning agent is necessary, as wastage in any form is not preferred.

3. A cleaning agent should be stored in a proper place and no misuse should be done.

DISTRIBUTION AND CONTROLS

The distribution is done as per the requirement of the desired area and everything is noted in the stock book. Issuing and receiving are done through supervisors to have effective control over things and to avoid pilferage, mishandling and misuse.

USE OF ECO-FRIENDLY PRODUCTS IN HOUSEKEEPING

'Mother nature' has given us so much and we must protect our environment. For preserving our environment, we should take ample care and try not to spoil/degrade our nature.

Being hospitality professionals, we can also contribute to the environment by using eco-friendly products as they get decomposed in nature.

Various hotels have started using these products, especially housekeeping personnel. It is suggested that eco-friendly products should be used as it will be a positive step towards saving our 'mother nature'.

CLEANING EQUIPMENT/MACHINES

Machine cleaning is being used more and more in hotels and institutions. It does a better job than manual cleaning and is less time-consuming. Also, it is cheaper than employing more labour and often, the only effective way of doing the job.

The following are the various types of vacuum cleaners you may find in use in hotels manual Equipment

1. **Brushes:** Brooms and brushes may be used for removing dust (i.e., for dry work) from a variety of surfaces, i.e., walls, floors, clothes, upholstery, etc., and may have bristles of animal, vegetable or man-made origin. Cobwebs may be removed as well as dust from cornices, ceilings and high ledges by the use of a wall broom. The head of which is soft and the long handle made of cane. Brushes are more frequently used for the removal of dirt, i.e., for wet work when the bristles are stiffer than those used for the removal of dust. This may be done by hand, using a scrubbing brush, floor cloth, detergent and hot water, or with a long-handled scrubbing brush (deck scrubber) using detergent and hot water; and for the efficient removal of the dirt, the soiled water must be picked up with a mop or vacuum drying machine

2.

Mops: Dry mops consist of ahead of various shapes and sizes, made from softly twisted cotton yarn or synthetic fibres and attached to a long handle. The synthetic fibres are electrostatic and attract dust. Some cotton mopheads are impregnated with a dressing which causes dust to adhere to the mop more satisfactorily. The large mops are known as **mop sweepers Wet mops** or **sponge mops** are used for cleaning lightly soiled floors in conjunction with a bucket, hot water and detergent. The mop consists of longer, coarser cotton yarn than a dry mop and a sponge mop is another type of wet mop. Both these mops, unless washed well after use, become unhygienic and as with dry mops if wrung by hand there is a danger of accidents.

Polish applicator mops usually consist of an oblong head attached to a long handle. This may be labelled for the type of polish used and the mophead then is not usually washed but replaced as necessary.

Squeegees are used to remove excess water from the floor and smaller ones are used in window cleaning.

2.   **Dusters and Mitts:** Dusters and mitts are used for the collection of dust from hard surfaces and are usually made of soft cotton or short-life material and mitts may be impregnated. Dusting is only an effective method of the removal of dust when the dust is collected on the duster. This entails the duster being used in the form of a pad with no loose ends to flick the dust about.

Damp dusting may prove more effective on some surfaces and is the only method used in hospitals. **Dusters** should be washed frequently.

Wet clothes should be absorbent and of a manageable size so that they can be wrung out by hand. They should be washed and dried after use to prevent them from becoming unhygienic. They may be colour coded according to the area or the purpose for which they are to be used.

Swabs may be of mutton cloth or other soft, absorbent material. They are used for wet work above the floor, i.e., washing paint, washbasins, baths etc. A short-life cloth, for example, cloth, is equally suitable but not so absorbent.

Floorcloths are made of COARSER COTTON material than swabs and are used for floors and pedestals when the use of a kneeling mat is advisable.

Dust sheets are made of thin cotton material, about the size of a single sheet, and maybe DISCARDS from the linen room, for example, thin curtains and bedspreads. They must always be kept clean and are used for covering furniture and during spring cleaning.

Druggets are made of fine canvas coarse linen, or clear plastic and maybe in the form of a CARPET SQUARE or A RUNNER. They are used to protect the floor during bad weather and redecoration.

3.   **Containers:** Buckets are normally made of plastic these days because they are lighter in weight, much quieter in use, and very much easier to clean than galvanized iron ones. Mop buckets on castors with wringer attachments are still usually made of galvanized iron.

7   **Polish applicator trays** are used when applying liquid polish to a floor with a polish applicator mop. They should be marked with the type of polish.

8   **Spray bottles** may be used to apply a fine spray of water or cleaning solution as required.

9   **Dustpans** are used in conjunction with a brush for the gathering of dust. Formerly they were of metal but now plastic ones are more usual and, to be effective, the edge in contact with the floor must be thin and flat.

Dustbins are often kept on the back stairs, in the maids'
service rooms or other convenient places. They used to
be made of galvanized iron and were very noisy but now
they may be of rubber composition or in the form of
refuse sacks, which are of strong disposable paper or
plastic and attached to a stand. Bins should be emptied
frequently and kept clean and sacks should be removed
when full.

Vacuum Cleaner

1.   **Small size vacuum cleaner (dry pick up):** Used
for room cleaning and is very effective; must be strong
as it is in constant use every day. Normally, comes with
attachments like crevice nozzle

– good for sides of chairs, a corner nozzle – good for
carpet edges, Venetian blinds attachment, a round brush
for upholstery and curtains. Used only for dry work.

2.   **Upright vacuum cleaner (dry pick up):** Suitable for the room but does not usually have attachments. In general, an upright type of machine is less flexible for room cleaning, as it is more difficult to clean under furniture. However, you will find them in use in many hotels. Again used only for dry work.

Wet and dry pick up machines: Similar to the wet ones but with the same machine one has the option of wet and dry use. One has to change the heads squeegee for wet use, carpets head for dry work. Furthermore, one has to change the filters – nylon for wet work and felt for dry work. This is a machine with dual purposes but one has to ensure that the staff is correctly trained in using it and adhere to the training. Otherwise, the parts may get damaged.

Tank type vacuum cleaner (wet pick up): This is a machine that picks up water. It is needed in hotels to pick up the dirty water after using the scrubbing machine. One uses a squeegee head to pick up the water. This can be fixed on the front or a flexible hose. Normally, such a machine is medium-sized. Sometimes one uses it on carpets after one has shampooed them.

Large tank-type vacuum cleaner (dry pick up): It is used in larger areas such as banqueting halls and restaurants as it is a large one and can work quicker than a small machine. There are some models that are huge and used in conference centres and other such places.

Cylindrical vacuum cleaner showing filters

3.	**Pile lifter:** It is a vacuum cleaner with usually two motors to make it extremely strong in action. The pile of the carpet is the hair of cut wool. (One can have loops which are uncut pile also). Due to the extra strong suction from the two motors, this machine grooms the pile, i.e., it makes it stand up better. One does not use pile lifters every day, but once a week in public areas and once in a month in rooms. Carpets with a deep pile react better to this machine. Pile lifters can be upright machines and tank-type also. There are attachments with the second motor that can be added to many smaller tank-type models.

4.	**Small hand vacuum cleaner:** This is used to vacuum upholstery, mattresses and can also be used for curtains, or fabric-covered walls.

Floor Maintenance Machines

These are machines which can scrub, shampoo, polish or buff floors. They are generally single disc machines, meaning the machine head is one disc. Some machines are available with three smaller discs, which rotate in opposite directions. There are different attachments that one uses for different functions SCRUBBING is done with either a scrubbing brush or with a scrubbing pad attached to the driving disc. The driving disc is made of small pins usually on one side so that pads do not adhere. One must also attach a water tank to the machine to hold the detergent and water and an outlet pipe to allow the flow of the liquid from the tank to the machine head. The machine has castors/wheels to make the machine movable.

Scrubbing pad used is made up of hard nylon generally black in colour.

Scrubbing pad is used for stripping floors.

POLISHING is done using only a polishing pad on the driving disc. Polishing pads are generally red and less hard than scrubbing pads.

BUFFING pads are usually beige or white. They can also be thinner than the other pads. One uses them with a driving disc.

SPRAY BUFFING is a method, where we use buffing pads and a spray attachment of polish attached to the machine, thereby replacing a fine spray all the time on the does not use a driving disc, this is only for pads. One can use the normal water tank with shampoo and water inside or there is another special kind of tank, which is a pressure tank and one uses this with dry foam type shampoo.

This creates a mousse and in that way, the carpets do not get too wet. Some shampoo machines have a wet vacuum built into the machine. This means all is done in one operation. The brushes of shampoo machines can be single disc type brushes or barrel type brushes that groom carpets pile very well.

There are shampoo machines, which spray a mist of shampoo solution on and the built-in wet vacuum sucks out the dirt and moisture. Usually, these machines have large and small size heads enabling one to use the small heads for upholstery and stain removal.

There are STEAMS SHAMPOOING MACHINES, which do a very effective in-depth cleaning. These machines are complicated and require a skilled operator.

UPHOLSTERY SHAMPOOING MACHINE is small size shampoos with a built-in vacuum cleaner. One can also use them for shampooing staircases that are carpeted.

HIGH-SPEED BUFFING MACHINES - The rotation of the single disc is very fast and one can use them for buffing. The revolutions are too fast for scrubbing or shampooing. Many hotels use them for spray buffing also.

INDUSTRIAL QUALITY MACHINES are always used in the hotel industry. Using domestic vacuum cleaners is not a good idea, as it would not withstand the wear and tear.

CARE OF equipment

Just as 'setting up and preparation for work' is important, so is 'closing down'. Equipment is expensive, proper care should be taken.

Procedure

Empty rubbish and linen bags

Strip trolley shelves and damp-wipe

Restock as required.

Vacuums

 Empty vacuum bags and replace damp-wipe the exterior of the machine, remove fluff from brushes, store neatly with flex (wire) loosely and tidily placed.

Brooms and brushes

 Remove fluff from brooms and brushes, wash in a warm neutral detergent, rinse and leave to dry. Store upside down to avoid distorting the bristles.

Toilet Brushes

 Wash toilet brushes in flushing toilet after use, weekly wash in hot water, 65°C, for ten minutes.

1. Wash mops and cleaning clothes in very hot water and neutral detergent, rinse thoroughly and hang to dry

Mop Buckets

 Wash and rinse mop buckets, turn upside down to dry.

Wringers

 Remove mop threads

 Clean rollers, castors

 Wipe down

   Pantry

Tidy pantry, store linen round side out. Damp wipe shelves as appropriate

 Mop floor.

Keys

Return keys and checklist to your supervisor before signing off duty.

www.ingramcontent.com/pod-product-compliance
Lightning Source LLC
Chambersburg PA
CBHW031314130726
47988CB00007B/2826